Python for Data Analysis

The Ultimate Beginners' Guide to Learning Python Programming Language, Pandas, NumPy, and IPython with Hands-On Projects

Zed Fast

Table of Contents

Introduction

Congratulations on purchasing *Python of Data Analysis,* and thank you for doing so.

The following chapters will discuss all of the parts that you need to know in order to get started with your very own data analysis in no time. There are a lot of different processes that you are able to use in order to enhance your business and ensure that others are going t0 notice the changes that you make. And to ensure that you cut out waste and get the results that you would like, you need to make sure that you are using the right method along the way. For most companies, working with the whole data science process can help, and a good data analysis is going to make sure that this is something that will happen for you.

In this guidebook, we are going to spend some time looking at the basics that come with a good data analysis. We will explore some of the basics of a data analysis, how to work with this process, some of the steps that are necessary in order to be successful with our data analysis, and even the reasons why the

Python language is going to work so well with the data analysis that we want to complete along the way.

From there, we are going to take things a bit further. We are going to look at some of the different tools and features that we are able to add to the process to ensure that we will be able to see the best results out of our data analysis. We will look at the importance of gathering the right data, why we need to spend time cleaning up the data and making it look nice, and even a bit about machine learning and how this fits into the picture.

Then it is time to take a look at some of the work that we are able to do with the different Python libraries. While there are a lot of amazing things that we are able to do when it comes to working with Python and ensuring that it will work the way that we want, adding in some libraries will be necessary to ensure that it is going to behave in the manner that we would like with data science. That is why we are going to spend some time looking at the most important libraries and extensions that we are able to focus on with this process, including NumPy, Pandas, and IPython.

To round out this guidebook and to help us end some of the discussion that we are working on along the way, we also need to take a look at what data visuals are all about and how they are going to fit into the process as well. these data visuals are going to make it easier to focus on what is going on with the work that we are doing in data science. Then we can end off with some of the practical uses that come with using data analysis on our businesses as well.

There are so many great things that we are able to do when it is time to work with data analysis. When we are able to put it all together, it is going to provide us with a lot of the benefits that we are looking for overall. When you are ready to learn more about how to handle your own data analysis, and how the Python language can help get this done, make sure to check out this guidebook to learn more and get started.

There are plenty of books on this subject on the market, thanks again for choosing this one! Every effort was made to ensure it is full of as much useful information as possible; please enjoy it!

Chapter 1: What is Data Analysis?

The first thing that we need to take some time to explore in this guidebook is the idea of data analytics. This is a great process that a lot of businesses want to explore and learn from, but it is important to understand what it is all about and how it fits into the world of data science. Often, data analytics is going to be the part that most people are going to look forward to when it comes to data science because it is the part where we get to play with some of the algorithms, and finally learn the patterns and more that come with all of this. With that in mind, let's dive into what data analytics is all about and why it is so important for our needs.

What is Data Analytics?

To start with here, data analytics is going to be the science of analyzing raw data in order to make conclusions and learn something from that information. Many of the techniques and processes that come with data analytics have been automated more into mechanical processes and algorithms that are going to work over the raw data to be used for consumption by humans.

The techniques that are often used when it comes to data analytics are going to reveal a lot of the metrics and trends that would easily get lost in all of the information that is out there. This information can then be used in order to optimize the processes and, if it works well, will help us to increase how efficient business or a system can be.

Understanding More of Data Analytics

We have to keep in mind that data analytics is going to be a very broad term that is going to encompass many diverse types of data analysis. Any type of information that we are able to get our hands on can be subjected to the techniques of data analytics in order to help us get insights that can be used in order to improve things.

Many companies are going to spend some time gathering up a lot of information. There is a ton of data out there that we are able to work with. And many companies hope that they are able to learn some valuable insights out of the process. The data analytics that we will focus on in this guidebook will help us to see what we can do with all of that data (and it is often going to come at us in a very large amount along the way as well). Since we are not able to manually go through hundreds of thousands of points, and sometimes millions of points, we need to use some of the work of a data analytics in order to take control and get this to work out in our best interests.

For example, we may find that a company of manufacturing will often record the downtime, runtime, and work queue for various machines and then will analyze the data in order to better plan out the workload that needs to be done. This helps to prevent one machine from overworking and another from not doing any work at all while it waits. It is one of the best methods to work with so that the machines are able to work at their peak capacity, or at least as close to this as possible.

Of course, we are also able to work with data analytics to help us with many more points than the bottlenecks in production. We are already seeing that there are a lot of gaming companies that will work with the idea of data analytics in order to set up some reward schedules for players, which ensures that most of the players out there active in the game. Content companies will use many of the same ideas of data analytics to keep the players clicking, watching, or re-organizing content in order to get more views or clicks in the process.

The process that is going to be involved when we talk about data analysis is going to include some of the following:

1. The first thing that we will want to do here is determining the requirements that we need t put on our data, or figure out how to group the data as well. there are a lot of ways that we are able to separate out this data based on what we would like to see it do, including age, income, gender, and demographics. We can also choose to make the data values may be numerical, or it can be divided up by category.
2. The second step that comes with data analytics is going to be where we spend some time collecting it. This can be done through a variety of sources, including computers, cameras, online sources, environmental sources and more.
3. Once the data has been collected, it is now time for us to organize it a bit more to ensure that we are able to properly analyze the information. All

of this organization can take place on some kind of form, including a spreadsheet, in order to help us learn how to handle the statistical data.

4. The data that we are working with is going to then be cleaned up before the analysis. This means that we are able to scrub and check it out to ensure that we don't find any errors or duplication and that there are no parts that are incomplete in this process as well. this one will ensure that we are able to correct any of the errors that may show up so that our data is not messed up and ruining the results that we will get from this either.

When the data is ready to go, we will be able to put it through an algorithm in order to make sure that it is set up and ready to go the way that we would like. When that is all done, we should get some good results that we can trust, and we can look through that to figure out the best course of action for our companies to work with.

This process of data analytics is going to be important because it is going to ensure that a business is able to optimize the way that they perform. Implementing this into the model that we use for business will mean that a company is able to really reduce its costs, simply by finding methods that are more efficient to get things done, and by storing large amounts of data as well.

A company is going to make use of data analytics in order for them to make some business decisions that are a lot better. And this also helps them to analyze the satisfaction and customer trends that are out there. And when this is done in the proper manner, it is going to help lead to some better and new services and products.

Types of Data Analytics We Can Use

Now that we have some of that information down, it is time for us to look a bit more at data analytics and what we are able to do with it a bit more. We are going to be able to break down this data analytics into four basic types, as well. Some of the most common types of data analytics that we are able to focus on will include:

1. Descriptive analytics: This is the kind that is going to help us to see what has happened over a given period of time. You would like at

something like whether or not the number of views on something has gone up or whether or not your sales were stronger this month compared to where they were last month.

2. Diagnostic analytics: This is going to be the kind that will focus a bit more on why something happened in the past. This could include a wider and more diverse input of the data, and you may need to work a bit of a hypothesis here as well. for example, you may use it to figure out whether the weather that year affected the sales you had. Or you can check whether the latest campaign you did for marketing is going to impact sales as well.

3. Predictive analytics: This is going to move on to what is most likely to happen in the near term instead. For example, maybe we will take a look to see what happened the last time that the winter was warm and then see how likely it is, by looking at the weather models right now, that we will have another warm winter. This helps us to predict how sales are going to be this year again.

4. Prescriptive analytics: This one is going to suggest a course of action that we are able to take. If you went with the option above and five

weather models guessed that the summer would be hot, then we would want to make sure that we take care of our business in the right manner. If a hot summer increased our sales the year before, then we need to add on another shift or handle it in another manner.

Data analytics are going to underpin a lot of the quality control systems that are in the financial world, and this is going to include what we are able to see with the very popular Six Sigma program. This is a program that a lot of companies are implementing in order to help them to reduce mistakes and wastes, and makes the business more efficient at what they are doing and so much more.

If you do not properly measure out something when you need it, whether it is the weight that you are using or the number of defects that happen per million in a production line, then it is going to be almost impossible in order to optimize it overall. And that is where data analysis is going to come into play as well.

Now, there are going to be some special considerations that we need to focus on when it comes to using data analytics. For example, we need to take a look at who is using data analytics in the first place, and if it is actually worth our time to get it all done.

There are a lot of different sectors that will use data analysis, and we will find that almost any industry is going to be able to handle and use this to benefit themselves. To start with, we will find that the hospitality and travel industry is going to use this because they need to be able to have a turnaround that is quick. With the help of the data analysis, this industry is going to be able to collect the data from a customer, and then figure out where the problems, if there are any, are found, and then how to fix them.

In addition, we are going to find that the world of healthcare is going to be able to use this as well. in many parts of the healthcare field, the use of high volumes of structured and unstructured data and uses data analytics to help make quick decisions.

In the same manner, like the options above, the retail industry is going to use a large amount of data in order to make some decisions and help them to handle the ever-changing demands that come form the shoppers.

The information that retailers are able to collect and analyze can help them to identify trends, recommend products, and even increase profits overall.

There are a lot of benefits that come with using data analysis. And we are going to spend more time searching through it and learning how to make this work for our needs as we go through this guidebook. There are many companies that are going to benefit when they choose to work with data analysis, and this is one of the best options to help us get ahead and see what the data is telling us about our customers, about the industry, and so much more.

Chapter 2: The Basics of the Data Analysis Process

Now that we have had a chance to work with the data analysis and we understand how this is going to work a bit better, it is now time for us to go through and learn a bit more about the actual steps that we need to use in order to help us finish this process. This process, along with a lot of the other options that we will talk about when it is time to work on data analysis, is not going to be all that simple, and there are a few steps that we are able to work with along the way as well. and that is why we are going to spend some of our time looking at more of the basics that come with data analysis and how we can complete this process in no time.

Setting Your Own Goals

The first step that we need to take some time to work with here is how to set your goals. It is so important for us to have goals that are simple, short, understandable, and measurable because it helps us to really learn more about how this process is going to work and what we are able to do with it as well. It will also make it easier for us to figure out what data we need to handle and where this process should begin before the data collection process is going to begin.

These objectives are going to be different for each company that would like to use them. And you may even choose to set them out in the format of a question as well. For example, maybe you are going through and notice that you are struggling a bit to sell your products. There are a number of questions that are relevant here that you are able to ask, including "How is the product from the competition different than ours?" "Are we pricing the products too high for our customers?"

Asking these questions and more is going to be important right away because the collection of data that we are going to do next will depend on the type of questions that you have, and can tell us what information we are trying to gather along the way as well. so, if you would like to answer the question about how the competition's product is different than yours, you would spend your time taking a look at the competition, asking the customers why they prefer the other product more than yours, and investigate how the two products are going to be the same or different from one another.

We can also spend some time looking at the question of whether the product is set at the right price. This will require us to go through and gather up data that will be about the cost of production, and details about how other products are priced on the market and then go from there with some of the work that you would like to accomplish.

As we can see with this one, the type of data that you will need to spend your time collecting is going to differ quite a bit based on what questions you would like to get answered as well. Data analysis is going to be a procedure that is lengthy and sometimes costly as well, so it is very important that we don't waste time or money-gathering up data that is not that relevant to us. And because of this, we need to make sure that, right from the beginning, we choose the right questions so that the data modeling team has a good of what we are looking for.

Figuring Out the Priorities for the Measurements

Once we have been able to go through and set up and define the goals that we would like to work with, then we have to go through and set it up to get our measurements figured out and know how we will measure all of this information. We also need to have a good idea of what methods we would like to use in order to measure all of this.

First, we need to have a good idea of what we would like to measure in the first place. Let's say that we want to start out with a question like, "How are we able to cut down on the number of employees without cutting down on the quality that we see with our products?" If this is our question, the data that we are going to work with will be along the line of how many people our business has as employees right now, how much we are paying these people each month, the other benefits that the employee is getting thanks to the company, and how much time the employees individually are spending on making the products. We can also take a look at whether or not there are any redundant positions that we can either get rid of or use with another form of technology as well.

As soon as the data that we need for the main question has been obtained, it is time to ask some of the secondary questions about the main topic form before. For example, we may want to go through and ask whether are some methods that will help us to increase the productivity that we have and whether all of the employees and potential showing through and being used well?

All of the data that we have been able to gather up to this point to answer the main question, as well as the secondary questions, can be converted into information that is useful. And when we do this well, you will find that it is going to be one of the best ways that we are able to assist the company when it is time to make some good decisions. For example, you may, based on the information that you were able to find, decide that it is time to cut out a few positions and use machines, or that you may want to change up the process that is being used.

The next thing that we need to focus on is choosing the right measurement. If you go with the wrong kind of measurement along the way, you will find that you will get the results along the way. The reason is that the data that you collect is going to really determine how you will do the analysis a little bit later on as well.

During this process, you need to as how much time you would like to take for the analysis of the project. At the same time, you also have to come up with the right units of measurement that you would like to use. For example, if you would like to be able to market the products that your company uses overseas, you would need to figure out whether you would like to measure the money you are receiving in profits in your home currency or foreign currency?

If we want to go through and work with the discussion of our employees that we did before, you would need to work with a different type of measurement. For example, you would need to go through and decide if you are going to add in things like the costs of safety equipment or their bonuses into account when you are doing this process.

Gathering Up Our Data

At this point, it is time to go through and gather up the data that we would like to work with. We need to go out there and find the right data, based on what we would like to measure, what our priorities are, and what our overall goals are as well. When we go through the steps that are above, you will find that it is a lot easier to cut through some of the noise, and not waste time, when you are ready to gather up the data that you need.

When we are going through this process of gathering up the data, there are a few things that we have to remember. First, we need to take a look to see if you already hold onto some of the data that is there based on your questions. There isn't any point in going through and searching around for the same data again or duplicating the data that you already have if it isn't necessary. You will also need to think about the method that you are going to use when it is time to combine together all of the information that you have at your disposal as well.

Maybe you have gone through and decided that you will gather up some of the information on the employees with the help of a survey. With this, we are able to think carefully about the kinds of questions that we would like to put into that survey before we ever send it out. You do not want to send out a lot of different surveys to the employees because they will get annoyed with it and won't fill them out. You need to make sure that you gather up all of the details that you need the first time.

The data preparation is going to involve a few steps as well, such as gathering up the data that you need, checking it out for accuracy, and then entering all of that information into a computer or database so that you can get that started for later. You will need to ensure that you have set up a good procedure for everyone to follow when it is time to log the data that is coming in, and for keeping tabs on it before you finish the actual analysis.

You might have some data that is coming in from different places, such as from interviews of employees, from the survey that we talked about, and even from observational studies. In some cases, you may even be able to go through and work with records for the payroll to make all of this work for you as well.

Remember that as we go through this process, we want to be picky about the data that you are taking in. You should take some time to check all of the information for accuracy as soon as you get it, and before it is logged at all. You may need to go back on occasion and ask for some clarification or figure out if you need more information to get things done. Doing this ahead of time is going to make a big difference in the success that you are going to see with all of this, as well.

If you have spent some time gathering up the necessary data in order to figure out whether or not your product is seen as overpriced, then it is time to double-check a few things as well. for example, you can check the dates that are included with this, since the prices and the spending habits of the customers tend to change on a regular basis, and can even fluctuate based on the season.

Data Scrubbing

Next on the list to work with is the process of data scrubbing or data cleansing. This is going to be the process that takes the most time, and it is where you are going to amend or remove any data that is incorrect or superfluous. Some of the information that you took the time to gather is going to be duplicated; it may be redundant, or sometimes it will be incomplete, and you will need to gather up some more information to get it done.

Because computers are not able to reason in the same manner as humans are able to do, we need to make sure that the data we add into the data analysis and the algorithms that we will use will be higher in quality. For example, a human would be able to pick out a zip code on a customer survey when it is incorrect by one digit, but the computer would not notice this.

It is going to help to know a bit about the main sources that we are going to see with dirty data. Poor data capture, such as typos, will be one of the issues, along with lack of standards across the company, missing data, different departments in the company using their own databases, and old systems that have data that is irrelevant and obsolete can be a few of the issues that show up here as well.

There are also a few tools that you are able to use to help with the process of data scrubbing. If you plan to work with a really large amount of data coming into the database on a regular basis, you will find that working with this kind of software will save you a ton of time. For example, because data has come in from many different sources and locations, including interviews and surveys, there is not always going to be a format that is consistent that we can work with here. We would need to use data scrubbing, and some of our software tools in order to change that and put all of our data into the same format to work with.

This process is going to take a bit, but it will involve identifying which sources of data are not authoritative, measuring the quality of the data, checking for some inconsistencies and incompleteness in the data, and even cleaning up the data while formatting it in the proper manner. The final stage in this process is going to be loading the cleaning information into the log or the data warehouse, as we may call it as well.

It is vital that this process is done and completed more as junk data because it is going to really affect the decisions that you make and how well the algorithm is able to help you out. For example, if you find that half or more of your employees are not responding to the survey at all, we need to look into that and take it into consideration. And finally, you have to remember that while data scrubbing is important, it is not something that allows you to get around good quality data in the first place. The higher the quality of data that you start out with, the better your analysis will go.

The Data Analysis

Now we are on to the fun part of the process. We have been able to collect the data that we would like to use, so it is time for us to take a step back and analyze it a bit more. There are a few methods that we will be able to use to make this happen, including a data analysis that is more exploratory, data visualization, business intelligence, data mining, and more. The first one is going to be one of the ways that we are able to get the sets of data analyzed, and hopefully, this is going to help us to get a better determination of the characteristics that are found in our information as well. in this manner, the data can then be used in order to test out the original hypothesis that we had.

Another method that we are able to use in order to help us when it is time to analyze all of the information that we have is with descriptive statistics. The data is going to be examined in such a way to help us find out what major features are present in it. An attempt by the analyst is going to be made to help make a summary of the information that we were able to gather during this time.

With the help of a descriptive statistic, the analyst is going to work with some simple tools to help them make more sense out of the huge amounts of information that we need to work with as well. The average or the mean of a set of numbers is something that we are able to use along the way here. This is going to help us to figure out the overall trend in no time.

Keep in mind though that while we can use this quite a bit, it is not going to be the most helpful when it is time for us to look at accuracy on the overall picture, so you may need to add in a few other tools to the mix to make this work. Sample size determination, for example, could be used to help with this. When you are ready to measure out the information that you have been able to gather from a large workforce, you may find, for example, that you will not have to work with each individual member just to get the accuracy that you need.

Along with our data analysis, we need to spend some time working on data visualizations, as well. This is going to be when we take that mountain of information we have been working with and analyzing along the way and put it into a form that is more visual, such as using tables, pictures, charts, and graphs, and then use that to see some of the more complex information that is found in our data. The main reason that this is used is to help us communicate the information in a manner that is easy and understandable. Even data that is really hard and complicated to work with can be put into a more simplified manner and understood by most people when we represent it in a visual manner.

In addition, these visuals are going to make the data easier to compare in the long run. For example, if you would like to figure out how well your product is doing when you compare it to the competition, you would want to look at a lot of information like the specs, the number sold the price, and more. You can put these into the form of a picture or a graph so that it is easier to assess the information and make informed decisions as well. You could read through this in the text form if you would like, but often the visual is easier to make quick guesses on as well.

The part of the data analysis is going to be very labor-intensive for this. Statistics will need to be contrasted and compared in the hopes of looking for differences and similarities. Different researchers are going to prefer some different methods as well to help them get all of this done. For example, they may find that it is easier to work with the software to get it done and to help analyze the data, and then there are going to be others who limit the software used to just helping them when it is time to manage and organize the information that they are supposed to work with.

Interpret the Results

Once you have had a chance to sort and analyze the data, it is time to actually go through the process of interpreting the data. You will now have a better method of figuring out if the information that you collected is done right and will be able to help answer the original questions that we had in the beginning. You would be able to see whether it answers the questions if it can help you to fight off the objections that you may have heard in the beginning. And are there any results in all of this that seem to be inconclusive or limiting along the way?

Depending on the results that you are getting in this process, you may find that it is important to conduct more research to get yourself set up and ready to go. You can also consider whether there are some new questions that were revealed that might have been hidden in the beginning? Could you answer the question better if you had ore data and research ready to go?

Sometimes the data that we are working with is going to be good for our purposes, and we will be set and ready to go with what we have. But we need to recognize that at times, we need to go back out there and search for more rather than just stopping because that is the easiest course of action.

Once you have been able to collect all of the data that you would like and you are certain that you have all of the information that is necessary to handle the situation, then it is time to interpret the results. If you worked with the right algorithms on your analysis, and you utilize the visuals that we talked about before, then you will be able to go through and figure out what is going on in the data, and then you can use that to make important decisions along the way for your business as well.

There are so many benefits that we are going to see when it comes to data analysis. But as we can see in this chapter, this is going to be a process that is more in-depth than a lot of people may be used to or have thought about in the first place. Learning how to do the data analysis in the right answers for your business and will ensure that you are able to get things done and learn how to beat out the competition in no time as well.

Chapter 3: Why Does Python Work so Well with a Data Analysis?

Now that we know a bit more about data science and what this is all going to entail for our needs, it is time to bring in the Python language and see why this is going to work so well for helping us to get things done in our data analysis as well. You will find that there are a lot of different coding options that you can make, and a ton of languages that can even work with the data analysis that we want to do. But you will find that when it comes to the ease of use and the power that you would like, then the Python library is one of the best options to choose along the way.

Let's start with a bit of background when it comes to working with the Python language. The Python language is going to be appropriated from Monty Python, which creator Guido Van Possum selected to indicate that Python should be a fun language to use. It is common to find some of the more obscure Monty Python sketches referenced in the examples of the Python code and some of the various documentation that we have with it as well.

For this reason, among some of the others that you are able to focus on as well, you will find that many programmers really love to work with Python. Data scientists that come from a wide variety of backgrounds, such as engineering and scientific backgrounds, may feel like they are a bit out of place when they start to handle data analysis and some of the steps that we were talking about above.

The good news is that Python is a good language to work with to handle this. The readability and some of the simplicity that comes with this language is going to make it easier to pick up and the number of analytical libraries that are dedicated to Python means that the data scientist, no matter which sector they are in, will be able to find the right package that they need, the one that is tailored to their needs, one that is freely available and can be downloaded in just minutes.

Because of the nature of Python that allows it to be a great general-purpose language and the extensibility of the language, it was pretty much a guarantee that this language was going to have a big explosion in the amount of popularity that comes with it. And it wasn't long before this language as turned around to work well in data analytics.

As a language that is known as a jack of all trades, Python is not going to be the best language to handle some of the statistical analysis that you would like. However, there are a lot of extensions that you are able to work in order to really make sure that you can handle all of this and can make sure that Python will be able to handle some of the work that you would like to do.

As is the with a lot of the other languages for programming out there, it is going to be the libraries that are available that will lead to some of the success of Python along the way. There are a ton of these libraries out there that you are able to use, and you will see that they are constantly growing. You will find that right now, the PyPI, or the Python Package Index, is going to contain most of these, and this is a list that is going to keep on growing over time as well.

When we work with the Python language, you will find that this is a language that was designed to have a core that is stripped-down and lightweight. In addition, the standard library has been built up with some tools to handle all of the tasks of programming that you would like. This is kind of a batteries-included idea that is going to allow the users of this language to quickly make their way down to the nuts and bolts of solving all of the problems that they have without having to sift through all of the function libraries out there and hope that they choose the one that is right.

One thing that a lot of programmers are going to like about the Python language is that it is free, and the software is seen as open-source. This means that it is possible for any company or programmer to go through and write out the library package that they need in order to extend out the functionality that is needed. Data science has been a really big beneficiary when it comes to some of these extensions, which is another reason why the Python language is going to be one of the best options to use in data science. You will find that the Pandas library, in particular, is one that is able to help us get our work done with data science in no time.

Pandas are going to be known as the Python Data Analysis Library, and it can help us handle all of the different points that are needed when it comes to doing data analysis. It is going to help us with all of the steps from importing the data that we need from Excel spreadsheets to processing the sets that are needed for an analysis that is on a time-series. Pandas are going to put all of the common data munging tools at your fingers right away. This means that even some of the basics like cleaning up the data and then the more advanced things like manipulation of the data can be done with the data frames that come with Python.

Pandas do need some help from a few of the other libraries that are out there, namely NumPy. This NumPy library was one of the earliest libraries that came out when it was time to work with Python and data science together. You will find that a lot of the functions of NumPy are going to be exposed in the Pandas library, especially when it is time to work with advanced numeric analysis.

Now, this is just one of the libraries that we are able to work in order to help us handle some of the data analysis that we would like to handle. There are a ton of other libraries that are available for data science when we work in Python, and this is part of what makes so many programmers fall in love with it in the first place.

Another great thing that you are able to enjoy when it comes to working with the Python language when it is time to handle data science is that it is going to have a base that is broad and diverse. There are going to be millions of users around the world who are more than happy to offer up some advice or suggestions when you get stuck something. This is part of the benefit. If you have gotten stuck on something along the way, then it is likely someone else has gotten stuck there too. You can use this community to help you grow and learn more and to ensure that you will be able to get through that problem and do better in no time.

You will also find that some of these open-sourced communities are going to be known for the policies that are open for discussion and will allow you to come in and ask the questions that you would like. But there are going to be a few that are not always the best for a beginner, and they will not like you coming in and asking a bunch of questions at that time either. Looking for the forum that is open and will be happy to have you come in and ask questions and learn will be the best bet if you want to be successful.

Python is usually an exception to the problem above. Most of the time, the trouble that comes with those communities will be found in other languages. This means that you will find a great group, whether it is a local meetup or online, where you can find experts and others who will help you to stumble through your new phase of learning and will make sure that you are able to catch on to the things that are most important when it comes to learning Python.

And since you will find that Python is definitely a prevalent option to work with when it comes to the community of data science, there are going to be resources out there that are very specific to working with Python in the field of data science as well. there are even some meetup groups out there that are just geared towards data scientists who would like to learn how to work with Python. And if you can't find a local group, you are sure to find a lot of online groups that can serve the same purpose as well.

As you can see, there are a lot of reasons to love the Python language, especially when you would like to handle some of the work that is necessary for data science and completing your data analysis. The Python language is easy to learn and has a lot of power at the same time, something that you are not going to see all that often when you are working with other coding languages that are available.

Many who start with Python worry that it is going to be too simple or too easy in order to handle some of the intricacies that show up with data analysis and data science. But it will not take long to see that the extensions that come in to help with this (and there are many) will allow you to really handle some of the work that you want to do in no time at all.

The extensions that are available to help out with data analysis are immense, as well. It may be true that Python is not able to handle some of these more advanced parts on their own. But when you are able to combine it together with some of the other libraries that are out there, including Pandas and NumPy, you will be able to handle all of this and more in no time.

And finally, the large community that is found with Python is going to be really good when it comes to working with data analysis and getting things done. While other languages may make it a bit tougher to get into if you are a beginner and trying to learn, the Python community is open and ready to help you learn more and get your feet wet in the process.

All of these benefits come together to ensure that you are able to really learn about data analysis and that you can learn how to use Python to make all of this a reality. This will ensure that you see the best results overall with this language and that it will end up working out the way that you want as well.

Chapter 4: Who Can Benefit from a Data Analysis?

The next thing that we need to spend a bit of time on here is who is able to benefit when it comes time to work with data analysis. Right now, it may seem like we are talking about an idea that is a bit more abstract than we would like. But we may worry that while it sounds all good and like it is something that we should take a look at, we may be worried that it is a waste of our time and that it will not help us to reach our goals.

A good way to take a look at data analysis, and really see the value that it is able to bring to you, and ultimately to the customers you are working with, is to see how other companies have been able to use this process in order to benefit themselves as well. That is why we are going to take a look at some of the different industries that have used this process of data analysis, and how they have been able to benefit from it overall.

Financial Services

The first place where we are going to see a bit of work with data analysis is going to be in financial services. There are a ton of big banks out there, along with other companies in the financial industry, who will work with data science, and even machine learning, in order to help them make smarter decisions and to help them keep the money and finances of their customers safe and secure.

There are two main reasons that this industry is going to work with the ideas of data science and may consider completing a data analysis as well. These will include identifying the insights that are important in the data and to help prevent fraud from happening in the first place. You will find that with the latter, when the algorithms of data analysis are given a lot of information about past activity that is fraudulent, then it will be better able to predict whether a transaction in the future is fraudulent or not and can prevent them from going through if they are wrong.

These insights are going to be so important when it comes to the financial industry. They will help these companies to figure out some new investment opportunities or will ensure that the investors will know the best time to trade to make the most money. Data mining is also going to help identify clients who are going to be higher risks to ensure that they are not going to give out money who are not likely to pay back their loans, and even to help them when it is time to pinpoint fraud, which is going to be something that helps out not only the business but their customers as well.

Health Care

Another thing that we need to take a look at when exploring who works with data analysis in the field of health care. This is a field that is quickly growing, and there are already concerns that those in the field will not be able to handle the workload in the future. Doctors will be overworked and will not have the necessary time to give to their patients, and the patients will be worried about receiving the care that is needed.

This analysis can really help out with this field, based on how they are used along the way. The idea of machine learning and data analysis is something that is really taking off in this industry, thanks to the advent of things like wearable devices and even sensors that can be used to help us assess the health of our patients in real-time. In a hospital that is busy and limited on staff, being able to put these on the patient and have the device record the information for us can save a lot of time and hassle along the way. In addition, you will find that they can be programmed to alert those in charge if something does go wrong or the patient's vital signs go down, so they can still get the care and attention that they need when necessary.

This is not the only place where we are going to see that data analysis is a good thing. For example, this can be used to help a doctor make a diagnosis a lot faster than they can do on their own, can help look for trends and red flags that catch diseases and illnesses faster, and so much more.

Government

Even the way that the government is run right now will benefit from the use of machine learning and a good data analysis. Government agencies, especially those that are found in utilities and public safety, are going to find that data analysis and a good amount of machine learning will be able to benefit them. This is especially true since they are going to need to be able to go through more than one source of data to find some of the insights that they need.

For example, it is possible to analyze some of the data that is found in sensors in the hopes of identifying ways to increase the efficiency of these agencies and make them easier to manage as well. They can even be used to help save money. Machine learning is also going to be used to help detect fraud and minimize the occurrence of identity theft along the way.

Retail Industry

This may not seem like a place where we are able to work with data science and machine learning, but you will find that the retail industry has a very large amount of data available. From surveys to information about the purchases that their customers have made at each visit, they will definitely have a ton of information that they can take ahold of and utilize in order to figure out what products to bring out next and so much more.

Think about the last time that you shopped online. Was there a recommendation that showed up while you were shopping, with things that you may be interested in based on some of the purchases that you made in the past? If this sounds right, then you already have a good idea of how machine learning can work. The company simply had to analyze the buying history that you have done in the past and put that to their advantage.

Many retailers are going to rely on this process in order to help them get more customers in the door, they will use it in order to capture the data, analyze it, and then use it to make a more personalized shopping experience, to help them out with some of the marketing that they would like to do, and to help out with things like customer insights, merchandise supply planning, and even optimizing the prices to make everyone happy.

The World of Oil and Gas

Another industry that is able to benefit when we take a look at data science is the oil and gas industry. There are many ways that this kind of industry is going to be able to ensure that they get the best results out of what they are doing along the way, and we will take a look at a few of them here.

First, we will find that this industry is going to be successful with machine learning and a good data analysis when it is time to find new energy sources that they can rely on. Some of the other ways that this industry is going to be able to benefit themselves is when they are able to analyze the minerals in the ground, predict when the sensors are going to fail, and even helping to streamline the distribution process so that it is more efficient and doesn't cost as much. There are a ton of ways that machine learning and data analysis are already being used in this field, and it is likely that the uses are going to keep growing.

Transportation

And finally, we are going to take a look at how we are able to use data analysis and some of the parts of machine learning in order to help out with the industry of transportation as well. you will find that when we are able to analyze the data that we have to find patterns and trends, we are working with some of the key points of the industry of transportation. This is because this industry is going to rely heavily on ensuring that routes are more efficient and in predicting some of the potential problems ahead of time in order to increase the profit that is seen.

The work of data analysis and modeling different aspects of machine learning is going to be important tools when it is time for some of these companies to get their work done. For example, all of these tools will be important when we are working with delivery companies, public transportation, and even some of the other companies that fit under this umbrella term.

As we can see already, there are a ton of different options that will come into play when it is time to handle data analysis and some of the work that we want to do with machine learning. We already took a look at some of the most prevalent options out there to help us gain a little bit better understanding of how this works and why it is so important to what we are trying to accomplish. With this in mind, we can already imagine what will happen with data science and a good data analysis in the future, as more companies decide to work with it for their own needs as well.

Chapter 5: Adding In Some Machine learning to Our Analysis

It is never a good idea to discuss some of the parts of data analysis without first taking some time to look more into machine learning and what this is going to be able to offer to us. Machine learning is going to help us to successfully finish some of the work that we want to do with data analysis, as it is in control overtaking our data and providing us with some of the insights that we would like.

To help us out here a bit, we first need to take a look at what machine learning is all about. For this one, machine learning is going to be one of the methods that we can use in data analysis that focuses on automating the analytical model building. It is going to be one of the branches that come with a computer science topic known as artificial intelligence. And it is going to be based on the idea that a network or a system is able to learn from the right data, and it will then be able to go through and identify patterns, make decisions, and handle some complex tasks, all without intervention from humans along the way.

How Machine Learning Came to Be

Thanks to some of the new computing technologies that are out there and ready for us to work with, you will find that the machine learning that we are able to do now is way ahead of what it was in the past. Remember that machine learning was originally from the idea of pattern recognition and that it had the theory that computers are able to learn along the way, on their own, without a programmer telling it how to do that tasks.

There were, at the time that this started, quite a few researchers who were interested in working with artificial intelligence, and they wanted to be able to make this process a bit further and see if computers are able to learn from the data as well. and that is where the beginnings of machine learning were starting to show.

Along the way, machine learning started to show an iterative aspect, as well. this is going to be an important part of how machine learning works and how the machine is able to learn along the way. This iterative aspect allows the model to get exposure to new data and learn more and adapt along the way as well. When machine learning is able to change and adapt, and it is used properly, the system that has this coding on it is able to learn from the computations in the past. With enough time and good data, the machine will be able to produce reliable and repeatable results and decisions.

This helps to remind us that data science is not a brand new thing to work with. But it is something that is gaining a lot of momentum at the moment, and this is going to mean that a lot of companies will want to work with it as well. while many of the algorithms that work with machine learning have really been around for a long amount of time, the ability to be able to automatically apply some of the complex calculations mathematically to the big data, doing it many times over and at a faster rate each time, is a development that is more recent.

Despite this, there are already a ton of ways that companies are using this to help benefit themselves as well. Technologies like the self-driving car, online recommendation systems, and fraud detection are already in place with many companies. And as we learn more about data analysis and machine learning, and start to see more of the benefits that come from it, we can guarantee that this is going to really explode and more technologies will be based on this in the future.

Why is Machine Learning Important?

From here, we need to take a look at some of the reasons why machine learning is so important to work with. There are a lot of reasons why there is such a big interest in machine learning today. And many of them are going to be the same as why data mining, and even the Bayesian analysis, are so important as well. Things like the growing volumes and varieties of data that is available, the fact that processing is a lot more powerful and affordable than it was in the past, and how we are able to find many options for our data storage needs will all come together and help us see why machine learning is so important.

All of these factors and more make it possible to automatically and quickly produce the models that we need. These models are going to help us to analyze bigger and more complex data, while also making sure that we can deliver results that are more accurate, and at a faster rate, than ever before. And this can no all be done on a large scale, one that we may not have known much about in the first place. And when we are able to build up these precise models, an organization is going to have a better chance of finding the best opportunities to go after, the ones that are the most profitable, while also avoiding the unknown risks that are out there.

There are a few things that we need to have in place in order to help us create a good machine learning system for our needs. Some of these are going to include the following:

1. The capabilities to prepare data.
2. Algorithms to help go through the data. Depending on the data that we are using, there needs to be both basic and advanced.
3. Processes that are both automatic or iterative.
4. Scalability to handle all of the projects that you would like to get done, whether they are big or small.
5. The use of ensemble modeling as well.

The Types of Machine Learning

Before we move on to another topic, we need to spend some time taking a look at the different types of machine learning. The two most widely used options are going to be unsupervised and supervised learning, but we will also take a look at reinforcement and semi-supervised learning as well. All of these are going to use different methods in order to get started with their work, but all of them can be important to helping us sort through our data and find those meaningful insights that we want. It often depends on the type of data that we will have, and what we want to do with the data, to help us figure out which learning algorithm that we would like to use.

The first type of learning algorithm is going to be known as supervised learning. These algorithms are going to be trained using examples that are labeled. This is often going to be done with an input where the desired output is known. For example, you could have a piece of equipment that is going to have various points of data that are labeled either F for failed or R for runs.

This kind of learning algorithm is going to work because it will receive a set of inputs, along with the right outputs along the way. Then the algorithm is able to learn because it will compare the actual outputs that it receives from the programmer with the correct outputs and will find the errors that show up in this as well. the algorithm can then modify the model that it is working with so that it does better the next time.

This kind of learning is going to use a lot of different methods in order to be successful. Through some methods like classification, prediction, regression, and gradient boosting, supervised learning is going to work with lots of patterns in order to help predict the values of the label on data that comes in later that is not labeled. Often we are going to find this kind of learning when it comes to applications where the historical data is going to help us to predict likely future events. It can anticipate, for example, when a transaction on a bank account is going to be fraudulent or which customers on an insurance claim are going to be the ones that cause trouble.

From there, we are going to be able to work with unsupervised learning as well. This is going to be the kind of data that is going to be used against the data that doesn't have historical labels at all. The system is not going to start out being told the right answer because it has to go through and figure out what is being shown on its own. The goal that comes here is to explore the data and then find some of the structure that is inside.

This kind of learning is going to work really well on transactional data. For example, it is able to go through the data that you have and will find customers who have similar attributes, ones that you are able to segment out and treat in a similar manner on your marketing campaigns. Or this kind of learning would be able to find some of the main attributes that help you to segment your customers from one another. There are a lot of options that you are able to choose from when it is time to work on this algorithm, including k-means clustering, self-organizing maps, and more.

Next on the list is going to be the type of learning that is known as semi-supervised. This type is going to be a good mixture of the two and allows us to get some of the benefits that come with both of them. This kind of learning is going to be used for a lot of the same applications that we see with supervised learning. But it is not going to rely on just labeled data to get it done. Instead, it will use a combination of both the unlabeled and the labeled data to help out with training. Usually, this means that just a small amount of labeled data is going to be used with a lot of unlabeled data because the unlabeled data is easier to get our hands on and is less expensive overall.

This type of learning is going to be used for a lot of options that you want to handle, including regression, prediction, and classification. And it is going to be useful when you find that the cost that comes with labeling is too high for us to have a training process that just relies on this labeled data. But you can still get the benefit of working with some labeled data along the way with this one.

And finally, we are going to take a look at something that is known as reinforcement learning. We are going to see this one a lot when it comes to navigation, gaming, and robotics. With this kind of learning, the algorithm will discover what actions are going to provide it with the best rewards, using a process of trial and error along the way.

There are going to be three main parts that need to show up in this kind of learning. We have to work with the agent, who is the learner, or the decision maker. Then we have the environment, which will be all the parts that the user is able to interact with. And finally, we send up with the actions which will be all of the things that our agent is able to do in this algorithm.

The objective that we are going to have with this one is that the agent will try to choose the best actions, the ones that will help to maximize the reward over a given amount of time. The agent will find that it is much easier to go through and reach their goal much faster when they are ready to follow a good policy. So the goal, in the long run, when it comes to reinforcement learning, is to help it find the right policy to work with.

All of these forms of machine learning are going to be important because they allow us to really work with the data that we have. As you go through your data analysis, you will find that there are a ton of different algorithms that fit into each of these learning types, so you will be able to find the methods that work the best for you and the data that you are working with overall. It is important to really learn about the algorithms, and what they can do so you can make sure you are setting yourself up for success when it comes to working on these algorithms and getting machine learning to do what you want.

When it is time to handle your data analysis, you will quickly find that machine learning is going to be an important part of the mix. It is going to be the part that helps us to actually go through and learn more about the data that we are handling, and to actually get the insights that we want. There are other steps that are just as important here, but we will find that by focusing more on the machine learning and getting the right algorithm, that all of those other steps are worth it and were really able to help us get the best results here.

Chapter 6: The Importance of Cleaning and Organizing Data

One of the steps that we need to spend some of our time on is the fact that we need to clean and organize some of the data that we want to use. If we send in our data to the algorithm and it has a lot of bad outliers, missing data, and duplicate content, we should not really trust the information that we are being given here. This is just asking the algorithm to provide us with inaccurate results because we are not providing it with the information that it needs. High-quality and organized data is imperative when we would like to work with this kind of data analysis in the first place.

A new survey of individuals who work with data analysis has found that most of these individuals spend a lot of their time massaging the data that they want to use, rather than mining or modeling the data. This survey took in the information of about 80 data scientists and was done for the second year in a row to learn a bit more about what this profession does and why it is so important as well. and there are a few highlights that we need to take a look at as well.

According to this information, the data scientist is going to spend about 80 percent of their work doing something that goes along with data preparation. About 2 percent of the time is spent building the training sets that they need. About 60 percent is spent helping to clean and organize the data, with another 17 percent of the time spent collecting the data that is needed to begin this whole process. Then another 9 percent is going to be done on data mining, four percent of building algorithms, and the rest is on other activities that are needed in order to get this process done.

This can sometimes come as a surprise to those who want to start working in this kind of industry. They are surprised that they are going to spend so much time just working through the data and making sure that it is clean and ready to go. Many assume that the majority of the time is spent working with the algorithms and finding out the insights. But since you are working with such a large amount of data, and you have to worry about it being nice and clean before you can send it through the algorithms that you would like, the majority of your time will be spent collecting the right data, and cleaning and organizing that data before even sending it through the algorithm that you would like.

Even though data scientists are going to spend so much of their time going through and looking to clean and organize that data, most of these professionals will agree that it is not that enjoyable. In fact, about 76 percent of data scientists out there view this kind of process as one of the least enjoyable parts of their work. And about 57 percent regard the part of the cleaning and organizing the data is going to be the least fun part, but another 19 percent say that the least enjoyable part is going to be collecting the data in the first place.

These findings are another confirmation that we are able to look at about a very well-known and lamented fact of the work experience for a data scientist. In 2009, the term "data munging" was something that started to catch on because it was supposed to describe the painful process that a data scientist has to go through when it is time to clean, parse, and proof your own data. Then in 2013, Josh Wills, who was then the director of Data Science at Cloudera, told in an interview, "I'm a data janitor. That's the sexiest job of the 21st century. It's very flattering, but it is also a little baffling."

This is really going to show us the big changes in data science, and how the idea of this job is so much different than what the reality is all about. There are plenty of people who think that this is a really hands-on kind of job, one that will allow them to do a ton of programming and have a lot of fun. And while you can spend some of your time working on things like this as well, and those parts are important, it is also important that we see that the majority of our time in this kind of profession is not going to be spent doing this kind of stuff. It is going to be spent working through the organization of our data.

What is interesting here, though, is that there are a lot of data scientists, despite not being that fond of working on the data organization and cleaning, even though this is the main thing they spend their time on, who wills till rate their job highly. In the same survey that we were talking about before, about 35 percent of these professionals gave their job the highest mark that was possible. And only 14 percent of these professionals at the time felt that they were being held back by their tool

What most of these data scientists wanted is more direction or support from their management or from the executive team they are working with, but most of them are happy with their jobs, and enjoy the work that they are doing. So, that is good news. Maybe with some tapered back thoughts on what this kind of job is all about, and how we are able to work with it too, you will find that this can actually be a really good job to work with, one that you are going to really enjoy along the way.

Now, why is data cleaning so important overall? We have already seen that it is necessary in order to get the job done because 60 percent or more of your job is going to be tied up in doing this process if you become a data scientist. So why is this such an important thing to work with overall?

The data that you are going to receive from online and other sources is going to be messy. It is going to come in with a lot of missing values, with duplicate content, with nothing being formatted in the right manner, and other issues as well. and while a few of these will not seem like that big of a deal, they really can make a difference in what your data is able to tell you. And when there ends up being a lot of these spread out through the data that you are looking at, it could lead to disaster when you try to run it through the algorithm later.

Remember that while machine learning and this data analysis can tell us a ton about the data, and will be able to run through the data faster than we are able to don our own, it is a computer, and it is an algorithm. It is not going to be able to go through all of that information in the same manner that we can. It will not notice that the data has duplicates or missing parts. It will just take the data that you send to it, and try to work with it the best that it can.

If there are a lot of mistakes and duplicates and other bad things, or low-quality data, found in your information, then this is going to lead to a lot of problems down the road. The algorithm is not likely to handle the data in the right way, and the results that you get are going to be inaccurate, and not all that good in the first place. You will get some insights and some predictions when it is all done because that is what the algorithm is set up to do. But these are not going to be all that accurate and will not tell you as much about the data, or the right things about the data, as you would like.

This is why cleaning the data is so important. It may not be the most exciting thing that happens with our data overall, but you will find that when we go through and clean up the data well, and we give it the time, and attention it needs, the insights and patterns that we are able to get out of our algorithms will be so much better. You will not find that the outliers or the duplicate content are going to mess with the results, and you can actually trust that you are getting what is best out of them each time.

There are so many benefits that are going to come with handling this part of the process. It takes a long time, and it may not be the most exciting part of this whole process. But it is one of the most important parts to ensuring that the algorithms are able to do their job well and that we are not going to end up with issues along the way either. Take your time when you reach this step, and it will be well worth it in the long run.

Chapter 7: Your Pandas Course

Now it is time for us to go through and look at some of the libraries that work well with the Python language, ones that are going to make sure that we are able to get the most out of some of the coding that we are doing in our data analysis. Remember that we brought up Pandas a little bit earlier, and talked about how it is one of the best libraries out there to help us get the results that we want and ensure that we are successful overall. And that is why we are going to spend some time in this chapter learning some more about how this library is able to work.

To start, Pandas is going to be one of the open-sourced packages of Python that will provide us with a ton of tools that are good for our data analysis. This particular package is going to be able to provide us with a few different data structures that we are able to use to help out with a lot of manipulation tasks on our data. It is also really great because it has methods that are specifically designed to help with data analysis, which makes it useful for some of our problems of machine learning and data science along the way.

The Main Advantages of Pandas

To start with here, we need to take a look at some of the great advantages that we will be able to see when it is time to work with the Pandas library. There are quite a few of these, and the fact that it is considered the best library to use for data science should already say a lot about how this one is going to work. Some of the advantages that we are going to see when it is time to work with the Pandas library in Python and for our own data analysis will include:

1. It is able to handle all of the different parts that we have in data analysis. As we have seen as we go through this guidebook, there are a number of steps that data analysis has to complete itself, and the Pandas library is able to handle them all.
2. The Pandas library is able to present the data in a manner that is suitable for this data analysis. This is going to be done thanks to the data structures of DataFrame and Series.
3. The package of Pandas is going to contain a lot of different methods that make data filtering more convenient to handle overall.

4. The Pandas library is going to have a variety of utilities that can come into play and help us when it is time to perform the Input and Output operations in a manner that is as seamless as possible. It is also able to handle any of the data that we try to bring to it, regardless of the format in question, including Excel, MS, TSV, and CSV, to name a few.

These, of course, are just a few benefits that we are able to see when it comes to working on the Pandas library. As you get some more time to really work with this process and learn more about how to handle the Pandas library, you will then be able to really make this work for your needs as well, and you will start to see some more of the benefits show up as well.

How to Install Pandas On Your Computer

Now it is time for us to take a moment and install Pandas so that we are able to use it for all of our data analysis needs. Keep in mind that the standard distribution of Python is not going to come with this module, so we will need to go through and install it separately if we would like to use it. The good news is that this is pretty simple to handle and will only take a few minutes in order to accomplish.

The nice thing about working with the Python language, though is that it is going to come bundled up with a neat little tool that is called pip. We are able to use this for a number of different tasks, but for our purposes here, it is going to make the installation of Python a little bit easier. To do this installation, we will need to run the command below:

$ pip install pandas

If you have already gotten the Anaconda program onto your system, you would just need to go through and use the following command below to help you get Pandas set up and ready to use on your computer:

$ conda install pandas

It is always recommended that you take the time to install the latest version of the Pandas package. However, if you do choose to go with one of the older versions because it works for your needs a bit easier, you can go through and specify this with the conda install command that is below:

$ conda install pandas = 0.23.4

The Data Structures in Pandas

Pandas are going to come with two main data structures that we are able to work in order to store our data. The first one is going to be the series, and then we have a DataFrame. The series is going to be similar to what we are able to see with a one-dimensional array. It is able to store any type of data that we would like, but the values of the Pandas Series is going to be mutable. Despite this should, the size of the series is immutable, which means you are not able to change it up.

The first element that is going to be found in the series will be assigned to the index of 0, while the last element is going to be N-1. The N here is going to be the total number of elements in the series. If we would like to take this information and create our own series in Pandas, we first need to make sure that we are importing the package of Pandas. We are able to do this with the import command of Python below:

import pandas as pd

Then we can go on to the next part of creating our own series. To help us get this done, we were able to invoke the method of pd.Series() and then pass the array doing the code that we find below:

Series1 = pd.Series({1, 2, 3, 4])

And then, we would end this by running the print statement so that we are able to see the contents that are found in the Series. The output you should have will have two columns in it. The first one is going to be the numbers that will start from our index, which is going to be 0. And then, the second column is going to be the elements that we decided to add to our series. The first column is going to also denote the indexes for the elements as well.

However, it is possible to get an error when we work on doing this, or when it is time to display our Pandas Series. One of the main reasons that this error is going to happen is that Pandas is going to look for the amount of information that you would like to display. This means that we need to make sure that we are providing the sys output information so that this error will not happen.

In addition, we are able to work with the DataFrame of Pandas. This is going to be more of a table that we are able to work with. It is nice to work with because it can take all of the data that we have and will organize it into rows and columns, which ensures that we are going to work with a two-dimensional data structure instead. Potentially, the columns are going to be of different sizes and types, and these can be mutable as well, which means that you will be able to modify them as needed.

To help us create the DataFrame that we would like, we get two options. One option is to start from scratch. This one takes longer to accomplish, but will ensure that we are able to get the exact data structure that we are looking for in the process. Or, we can choose to convert other structures of data such as the arrays that we see in NumPy, over into a DataFrame.

How to Import the Data

The next thing that we need to focus on here is how we are able to import the data that we are working with. There are a lot of times when a data analyst will need to work with Pandas in order to analyze some of the data that has been stored in another file, usually a CSV or an Excel file. This is going to be an important step because it is going to require that we are able to open up and import the data from these other sources over into Pandas.

The good news is that Pandas does allow us to work with this, and it also provides us with a lot of different methods that we are able to use to help us load the data from a lot of sources over into a DataFrame that we talked about before. This will ensure that it is in a format that we are able to read through and understand easily.

First, we need to explore how we are able to do this with the CSV file that we have. To start on this one, though, CSV is going to stand for comma-separated value, which is just going to be a text file that will have all of the values separated out with a comma. Since this is a standard that is known and used quite a bit, we are able to set up our Pandas library so that it will read this file, either in part or we can have it read the whole file.

It is also possible for us to go through and import some of the data that we have from an Excel spreadsheet if that is easier for us, and that is where our data is going to be found. In addition to the read_csv method that we are able to work with above, Pandas is going to have a function that is read_excel in order to handle all of the Excel data that we have and will put it into a Pandas DataFrame as well.

How to View and Inspect Data

The next thing that we need to take a look at is how to view and inspect the data that is necessary. At this point, we have taken a look at how to load the data, but we need to actually take a look at how to view the data and see what is there. For this, we need to take a look at the data frame and see if it is organized and will do what we want.

Running the name of our chosen data frame is going to give us the full table. If this is what you are hoping to get your hands on, then this is a good place to get started. But you are also able to get the first number of rows that you would like with the help of the code df.head(n), or you can even get the end of it as well with the help of the df.tail(n). there are a lot of different codes that you can use in order to see the specific parts of the table that work the best for your needs, but some of the options will include:

1. Df.mean(): This one is going to return the mean of all the columns that you are working with.
2. Df.count(): This one is going to return the number of non-null values that are found in each of the columns that are in your data frame at that time.
3. Df.corr(): This one is going to return to us the correlation that is there between all of the chosen columns inside of that particular data frame.
4. Df.max(): This one is going to return the highest value that we are able to find in each column.
5. Df.std(): This one is going to return for us the standard deviation that we are able to find in all of the columns that we are working with.

6. Df.median: This one is going to return the median that we are able to find in all of the columns.
7. Df.min(): This one is going to help us to see what the minimum value is in each of the columns that we are able to work with.

From there, we are going to be able to take some time to look through the data and even select the data that is the best for us to use at that time. One of the things that you may notice, especially if you have worked in data science and data analysis for some time, is that Pandas is going to help you select the data that you would like to compare in a manner easier than other options. You simply need to select a column and then return a column with a label of col as a series. You can even do this with a few columns if that works better. And if you are working with more than one column here, you will find that these new columns will come back as a new DataFrame in the process.

If you would like to select the first row and look this one over, you would be able to work with the code of df.iloc[0 :]. And if you would like to make sure that you are selecting the first element that is in the first column, you would want to run that code as df.iloc[0 0]. Remember that the first row or column in the frame is going to always be 0 and then you can number on from there. These can always be done in a variety of combinations, so do a bit of experimenting and see how this is going to work for your needs.

Data Cleaning

As we can see through here, there are a lot of different things that we are able to do with our data, and Pandas is able to help us get all of this done in a quick and efficient manner. And you will find that it is also able to help us work with some of the data cleanings that we discussed as important in the last chapter as well. Pandas have a lot of the tools that we need in order to get that data organization and cleaning process done in no time.

To start, it is able to help us put the data into a database, helping us to sort through it and understand what is there, what is missing, and more. It can help us to filter out the data, sort the data, and even group the data in the manner that we would like. And it is a good tool for helping us to really learn how to separate out the information and figure out the best way to use it in our chosen machine learning algorithms.

Pandas are going to be a really useful kind of library that we are able to work with, especially when it is time to handle Python and data science together. There are a lot of functionalities that come with Pandas that will make our whole data preprocessing project a lot easier than before. We took a look above at some of the main parts that come with the Pandas library and how we are able to use this for our needs. But there is so much more that we are able to do with these if we so choose. You will find that the Pandas library is really a great option to work with, no matter what your overall project is about.

Chapter 8: Your Ultimate NumPy Course

Another library that we need to spend some of our time on here is going to be the NumPy library. This is a good library to learn about when it comes to Python and data science because you are not going to get very far with any of the other libraries without this one. This NumPy library is set up to be the basis of a lot of the other libraries, and many of them rely on the NumPy array in order to get things done overall. With that in mind, we need to take a closer look at the NumPy library and all of the neat things that we are able to do with it as well.

To start with, NumPy is going to be an open-source package that comes with Python. It is going to be used for a lot of the numerical as well as scientific computing that we would like to get done. And many times, it is going to be used when we want to compute the necessary arrays in a more efficient manner. We are able to use this one including Python and C.

Many times this library is going to be added to the computer as a package from Python, and it is mostly associated with Python because NumPy is going to stand for Numerical Python. There are a lot of options that we are able to pull out when it is time to work with this library, but often it is going to be used to help us process homogeneous multidimensional arrays.

Another benefit that we are going to see when it comes to using this kind of library is that it is going to be seen as the core library when it is time to work with scientific computations. Because of this fact, it is going to be important with a lot of the scientific programming options that you would like to do along with the Python language, including scientific programming, machine learning, statistics, and more.

NumPy is also able to provide us with a lot of good functionality since it is well written and is able to run in a really efficient manner. Many data scientists are going to use this in order to help them perform some of the mathematical operations that are needed, including those that they would like to finish on a contiguous array, which is similar to the method that you would do on arrays in the C language, if you have worked with this as well. To make this a bit easier to grasp, this library is often going to be used when we need to manipulate some of the numerical data that we are working with.

Understanding NumPy Overall

You will quickly find that NumPy is one of the most widely used libraries out there when it comes to the Python language and data science. Many of the things that you are going to do in data science and data analysis will need to be done on matrices and large-size arrays, and a lot of heavy numerical computation is necessary in order to take the data that you are working with and get the information that you need, and that is the most useful in the process. And all of these are functions that the NumPy library is able to help us out with.

It is often seen as one of the most basic libraries to focus on when you want to complete the data analysis, and many people barely give it any attention. But there are definitely a lot of features that are found with this option, and you will not be able to get some of the stronger libraries to work well if you are not careful about using this one as well. Many of the more advanced libraries, including Pandas that we talked about before, are going to be dependent on the arrays of NumPy to do even the most basic of their outputs, so it is important to know this language, and often you will need to import it to work on some of your programs.

NumPy can take it a bit further, though. It is a good language that will provide all of the functions that developers need when it is time to do both basic and advanced numerical and mathematical and statistical functions with fewer lines of codes than other options. This is done thanks to the array, which is going to be more homogeneous than some of the other options you can choose in other languages, and we have to work with them any time that the elements of our array need to remain as the same type.

If you have spent any time working with Python in the past, you will find that the arrays in NumPy are going to be similar to the lists that we are able to see in Python. However, the arrays here are going to be faster. The lists, on the other hand, are going to show us more flexibility because, in the arrays, you are only able to store the same type of data in each column.

The Features of NumPy

The next thing that we need to take a look at here is some of the features that are going to come with the NumPy library. There are so many things that you are going to like about this coding library, and even if you think it is basic or that it is going to be missing out on some of the important parts that you need, you should not discredit this as a great option. Some of the features that we need to really pay attention to when deciding to work with this library and have it in our arsenal will include:

1. It is able to reshape the arrays that are being used at that time. And because of this, we are able to use Python as an alternative to the MATLAB option that is very popular, but sometimes hard to work with.
2. There are various functions of the arrays that we can choose when we work with this language.
3. The arrays that we can get from NumPy are going to be very versatile, and a lot of the other languages that are out there will rely on these to get their work done as well. these arrays are going to be homogeneous and multi-dimensional.

Ndarray is going to be known as ndimensional arrays and can be used in many situations when coding.

Why NumPy Makes Work Easier

You are easily able to go through and use the NumPy library in order to create arrays that are homogeneous and then use these in order to do a lot of operating son. We are going to take some time here to look at a few of the options that we are able to do. For example, these arrays can help us to import by using the following command to get NumPy imported as NumPy

NumPy n-dimensional array

One of the features that come with this library that is the most important is that the n-dimensional array is going to be the nd-array. The number of dimensions that we are going to find in the array is going to be nothing outside of the array rank, so keep that in mind.

From here, we are also able to create our own NumPy array if we would like. This can be a good thing because it ensures that we are not stuck just using the arrays that are available in the system, and we can make some of the different parts that are needed in our own coding along the way. The coding that we are able to use in order to make sure that we can create an array when we need it is below:

```
arrA = numpy.arange(3)
```

This is going to work in a manner that is similar to what we see with the range in Python. When we type in that program with the help of the NumPy library, we will find that it is going to create a new array for us, and that array is going to be to the size of 3.

Why Should We Use NumPy

We can also take some time here to explore why the NumPy library should be used in the first place. There are a lot of other libraries out there, and it is likely that you have already noticed that we talk about the Python list a bit and how it is somewhat similar to the array that comes with this library. With that in mind, why would we want to bring out another library and get caught up in all of the work that this is going to bring us along the way as well?

There are actually quite a few reasons that we would want to work with the NumPy array instead of the Python list, even though the two of these are going to seem really similar to one another. The first one is that there is less memory that is being used with the array. This may not seem like a big deal when you just work with a little bit of data. But when you have a huge amount of data that you are trying to store on your system and you are trying to do all of the work that comes with data science, you need to preserve as much of the memory that you can on your computer.

Another benefit is that the array is faster when it performs. When you are sorting through millions of points of data, potentially, you want something that is as fast as possible. And when there is this much data that we are working with, a little bit of a delay is going to really add up quickly. If you want to be able to get through the whole process as quickly and efficiently as possible, you would need to make sure that you are working with this array rather than the list. For smaller projects or for learning how to work with the Python programing language in the first place, the list is just fine.

And finally, we will find that these arrays are going to be pretty convenient to work with overall. They are simple, they will be able to handle all of the data that we are trying to work within this kind of process, and they can make the work of a data scientist just that much easier overall. You will find that when you need to get the work done quickly and you do not want to mess around with waiting or something that is overly difficult, that the array from NumPy is going to be one of the best options to choose.

Among some of the programming languages that are out there, you will find that Python is really trending when it comes IT field and more. This is going to ensure that you are able to get a lot of the work done that you want and can increase your chances of finding the career that you would like. In fact, the number of careers that are growing in Python right now is insane, and if you want a field in IT, you will find that Python is one of the best places to go for it.

We have already taken a look at some of the benefits that come with the Python language and how well it is able to work with some of our goals in data science and in completing the data analysis that we would like. It is also a great way to ensure that we will be able to work on some of the machine learning algorithms that are so important to ensuring that our data is well taken care of and that we can actually see some of the results that come with it.

As you get more into the process of data science and data analysis and you throw in a bit of machine learning, you will find that this is going to really need to rely on a few extensions and libraries to the Python language. Python is amazing and can do a lot of things for us along the way, but it does need some help with those more advanced features. And this is where the NumPy array is going to come into play as well. it has a lot of the basic features and more that we are looking for, including the arrays, and many of the other, more advanced libraries, are going to rely on this to get their own work done too.

Chapter 9: Adding IPython to Your Arsenal

Now it is time for us to learn a bit more about another feature that we are able to use along with the Python language, and this is going to be known as IPython. If you have already been able to download the Python language and you have worked on it a little bit you have been able to start up the Python interpreter simply by typing in the command of "python" on the terminal of the computer you are working with.

When the interpreter has been able to load itself up, you are able to run all of the code that you would like with Python using this interpreter in the terminal. Although this is going to be really helpful to work with, the Python interpreter is going to have some limitations to work with as well. For example, the Python interpreter is not going to provide us with some features like highlighting the syntax, completion of tabs, proper indentation, and so much more that can make coding better.

This is where we are going to run into the idea of IPython. This is going to be one of the alternatives that you are able to work with compared to the interpreter of Python. It is going to be an interactive shell that we are able to use to help out with some of the Python work that we would like to do. It is also going to provide us with a lot of useful features that are not found in the interpreter that is the default in Python. And that is why we are going to spend some time looking more into this shell and what all we are able to do with it to meet our needs.

Where Can I Get IPython?

The first thing that we need to take a look at is how we can find this shell and what we are able to do with it. There are actually two methods that we are able to work with when it comes to installing this program on your computer. If you are already using Python and it is already installed on your computer, then you will want to work with the Python package manager, or pip, in order to get the IPython shell using the following command:

pip install ipython

Now, we are going to recommend that you install this shell with the help of the Python Anaconda distribution. When you install the Python program with the help of Anaconda, then you will find that the IPython shell is going to install automatically as well. bit if you install it through Miniconda, which is just a smaller version of Anaconda, then you will need to install this shell using conda, which is the Anaconda's package manager for some of the packages that are available for data science. We are able to do this using the following command to make it a bit easier:

conda install ipython

These are going to include some of the basic things that you are able to do when it is time to install this process. You can go with a few other methods if you would like, but these are nice and simple to work with and will be able to handle all of the work that you would like to do in the process as well.

How to Work with IPython?

The next thing that we need to take a look at here will be how to work with IPython. At this point, we should have the right steps that are needed in order to get the IPython program installed on the computer. You will find that this shell is not going to be too different from working with the default shell on Python, and that can make it easier to learn how to work with this one overall. To use this, you can just type in the command that is below into the terminal of your computer:

iPython

After we have taken the time to type in the command above you will find that the terminal is going to show us some information. This terminal in specific is going to provide us with a bit of detail that comes with IPython, including the version that we are working with, a description of this shell, and some of the commands that we are able to enter that can help us to get things set up and ready to go.

And that is all that there is to this process. When you get to this point, you have already been able to load the IPython interpreter. And that means that it is time for us to look at a few of the features that are going to come with this shell and that we are able to use for some of our own needs as well.

The Features We Need to Know of IPython

Now that we have had some time to install this shell, it is time to take a look at what this interpreter is going to provide to us, and some of the reasons that this one is seen as an improvement over the default interpreter that is there. That is why we are going to take a look at some of the different parts that are going to be seen when it is time to handle this process.

First, IPython is able to help us run some of the native shell commands. When you decide to run the interpreter, this is usually going to come to us with some of its own built-in commands. These commands are going to collide with some of the native shell commands that you will see along the way.

For example, you may find that if you were able to start up the interpreter that comes in Python, and then you type in "cd" after the interpreter has had time to load, then you are going to see that there is an error that shows up in the terminal. This is going to happen because the interpreter doesn't recognize what this command is all about.

The interpreter is going to be this way because the command "cd" is going to be native to the terminal of your computer, but it is not going to be native to the interpreter that we are using in Python. This is no longer a problem when we are working with IPython, though. This shell is going to support some of the native commands of the shell including command history, ls, and cd to name a few.

Another benefit that we are going to see is the idea of syntax highlighting. For a lot of people, this is actually one of the first things that you are able to notice about this shell. This means that it is going to work with colors to help you to differentiate some of the different parts that show up in the Python code. This makes it easier to see what is going on, and to read through some of the information that is there.

We can also focus on the idea of the proper indentation with this one. If you have worked with the Python language before, then you know that it is going to be focused quite a bit on the indentation and the whitespace that is going to show up. With the original interpreter, this is harder to work with than it may appear. But with IPython, it is going to recognize this and will automatically help us provide the right indentation when you type in the code that you would like to use in Python.

The tab completion that we want to handle with this one is going to be a good feature of the IPython shell. This is going to help us to work with the process and will put all of the codes in the right place along the way. You are also able to use the arrow keys, the up and down on the keyboard, in order to navigate through the methods and then select the one that you would like to use. There is also the option of starting to type in the name of the method that you would like to use, and then complete all of this with the Tab part. This is a much nicer option over the default interpreter that is available there.

The next feature that we are going to enjoy when it is time to work with the IPython shell compared to the original is going to be the documentation. The tab autocompletion that we talked about before is going to be useful because it is going to provide you with a list of all the methods that are possible based on the specific module that we are working with. With this vast array of options there, it can seem overwhelming, and like it is too much to handle overall. You can also run into situations where you wonder what a specific method is going to be able to do for you. Once again, you will find that the IPython shell is able to handle all of this.

Pasting blocks of code can be another benefit or feature that comes with this kind of shell, and it is a good option to work with when you would like to get this shell to paste a large amount of code in one place. You are able to grab onto any block of code in Python, copy it, and then paste it over into IPython. And the results that you are going to get with this will be code that is properly indented inside of the interpreter that you are working with.

As you can see, there are a lot of benefits that you will be able to get when it comes to working with the IPython shell, especially when it is compared to the regular or traditional Python interpreter that we have talked about before. This is really going to provide us with a lot of improvements compared to the default interpreter that is found in Python.

There are a lot of improvements that are seen with the IPython option, including syntax, highlighting, proper indentation, documentation, and all of the other options that we have talked about int his chapter so far. With this shell, you also get the benefit of working with the JUpyter notebooks to create some of the reports that you need, the ones that contain some code, charts, and more that are life.

If you really want to be able to work with the Python language to help you with things like a good data analysis and to do some work with the help of computing, then you need to consider expanding out from the regular option of Python and its shell and instead consider working with IPython. With some of these more complicated tasks, you will find that this is really a tool that is going to be useful and will ensure that you are able to get the best benefits out of the process as well.

Chapter 10: Using Visuals to Finish the Project

Before we are able to end some of our discussion when it comes to working with a data analysis process, it is important to take a look at how we are able to look at the data and understand what is inside of it. You will find that there are a lot of benefits to working with the data analysis process, and we have taken some time to explore all of the different parts that come with it. But before we can end, we have to look at how we are able to work with the charts and graphs that are present in this, and how they can really help us to see some of the more complex relationships that are found in some of the data that we are able to work with.

To keep it simple here, data visualization is going to be the way that we can present our data, and all of the findings that we have, in a graphical or pictorial format that is easy to look at and understand. It is going to enable some of the key decision-makers of a company to really see some of the analytics that you did in the other steps, but the information will be presented in a more visual manner, making it easier for all to really grasp the difficult concepts that are there or find some of the new patterns as well.

When you take the visualizations that we are talking about here and make them more interactive, and even mess with them a little bit, you can really take this concept to the next level. It can help us to use technology to help drill down into the graphs and charts that we have for some more details and can be a great way to interactively change what data you are able to see, and how we are able to process it as well.

Why Are These Visuals Important?

You will find that there are a lot of benefits when it comes to working with data visualization overall. Due to the way that most humans are able to process the information that they are working with, you will find that it is often easier to work with graphs and charts in order to visualize a lot of information or a lot of complex data. This is a much nicer, and easier method, compared to working with reports and spreadsheets at least.

Compared to the reports and spreadsheets that are available, you will find that data visualization is going to be easy and quick, and one of the best ways to convey the concepts that you would like, and the important parts of your data, in a manner that is universally easy to understand. And you are able to do some experimenting with them in order to see what the different scenarios are like, with a few slight adjustments along the way.

There are a lot of ways that we are able to work with data visualization as well. Some of the other methods that we are able to work with will include:

1. Identifying the areas that are most likely to need our attention or that could use some improvement overall.
2. Clarify which factors are the most likely to influence the behavior of the customer.
3. It helps us to understand which products we need to play and where they should be placed.
4. It can make it easier to predict the sales volumes that we are able to work with during different times of the year.

As we can see already, these visuals are going to come into play and will ensure that we are able to really understand some of the complex relationships that are found in the data that we are working with. You will be working with a lot of data and information when it comes to handling a data analysis, and you do not want to leave the work up to chance when you get to this point. Working with some good data visuals to make it easier to understand that data and what it is trying to tell you will be very important when it is time to get started on this process overall.

How Can These Visuals Be Used?

There are a lot of ways that we are able to work with these data visuals, and that is part of what is going to make them so unique. To start with, these visuals are going to be a great way to help us get a better comprehension of our information in a fast and effective manner. When we work with some of the graphical representations of our business information, it is easier to see the complex and large amount of data that we have in a clear and easy to understand manner. And when we are able to do this, it is easier to draw some good conclusions form that information.

And since the data is going to be easier to analyze when it is in the graphical format, compared to what we would do if we needed to analyze it in a report or in a spreadsheet, it is easier for the business to answer questions and address some of the major problems that they are facing in a timely manner, without the wrong information or having to worry that things are not lining up the way that they should.

Another way that we are able to work with when it comes to these visuals is that it can ensure that we will pinpoint some of the emerging trends. When a business is able to use these visuals to help them pinpoint some of the trends that are coming up in the market and in their own business, it is going to help you to gain a good edge over others in the industry. And this is always going to help to improve your bottom line.

When you work with these visuals, you will be surprised not only at how easy it is to understand the data and look it over, but also how easy it is to spot some of the outliers that are present, the ones that are going to affect the quality of the product or even your customer churn. And this is going to allow you a chance to address some of the issues that may come up before they turn into problems that you and your business are not able to handle.

The next benefit that we will see with these visuals is that they will make it easier to identify some of the patterns and relationships that are found in all of that data along the way. Even some of the really complex data, and even when there is a ton of data, it will start to make some more sense when we are able to present it in a more graphical manner, rather than in a report. When we are able to use these graphs and charts, it is so much easier for us to really find the parameters and see how they are closely correlated.

Of course, you may find that in some situations, the correlations are going to be easy to see, and we will be able to find them and understand them without having to work with the visuals at all. But other times, these are harder to find, and you could spend hours looking over the report without any kind of luck along the way. Being able to identify these relationships is going to be a good way to help organizations to focus more on areas that are going to be the most likely to influence their most important goals overall as well.

And finally, we will find that working with these visuals is a great way to communicate the story of the data to others. Sometimes, the people who need this data and information the most are not going to be data scientists, and sometimes, they need a method that is easier than the scientific and technical stuff to help them out with understanding what is in the data. And this is where the data visuals are going to come into play.

Once a company or a data analysis is able to uncover some new insights from the visual analytics that they have, the next thing that they need to be able to do is really communicate these insights and patterns to others. Using graphs, charts, and some of the other representations that are visual of the data is going to be such an important step because it is going to be easier to understand, is more engaging, and will ensure that the message is getting across to the right people in no time.

How to Lay Some of the Groundwork

Before we go through and start implementing some of the parts that come with these visuals, we need to follow a few steps to ensure that we are getting it all set up in the right manner and to ensure that it is going to work in the manner that we would like. Not only is it important at this point for us to have a good grasp on the kind of data that we are working with, and what is found in that data, but we also need to have a good understanding of the needs and goals that we have, and what audience we are trying to reach as well.

Preparing your company for the technology that is needed to help with data visualization is going to have a few requirements along the way. And these will be:

1. We need to have a good understanding of the data that we would like to turn into a visual. This means that we need to also know a bit about the uniqueness, or the cardinality, of the data values that we have, and the size.
2. We need to really determine what we are trying to visualize in this process, and what information we are hoping to show off and communicate to others in the same visual.
3. We need to have a good understanding of our audience, and we need to know ahead of time

how they are likely to process some of this visual information as well.

4. We need to make sure that we are choosing the visual (and there are quite a few of these that we are able to choose from (that will be able to convey the information in the simplest and the best form so that it is easier on the audience overall.

Once you have been able to go through and consider these different points and answered some of the initial questions about the type of data that we have, and the audience who is most likely to consume this information, then we need to be prepared for how much data is going to come through. Big data, which is the most often used when we are talking about data analysis, is going to bring along some new challenges that we need to face, and figuring out how to complete the visual is going to be important here.

Chapter 11: Real Applications of Data Analysis

Now that we have had some more time to talk about what a data analysis is all about and how we are able to add it all together to get what we want out of all that data in the world, it is time to take a look at some of the real-world applications of all of this, and how we are able to use this for our own benefit as well. There are a ton of benefits to working with data analysis, and you will find that almost every industry out there is going to be able to benefit from using this as well. some of the best applications of this data analysis that we are able to work with will include:

The Financial World

The world of finance can definitely benefit from the user of a good data analysis in order to get things. For example, the SEC, or the Securities Exchange Commissions, is always working with big data, and using that in analysis, to help monitor the activity that is happening on the financial market overall. The SEC is right now working with network analytics, and even the idea of natural language processors, to help catch on to some of the illegal trading activities that could happen on the financial market in order to shut these down a bit faster.

Big banks, retail traders, and hedge funds, along with some of the other big boys in the financial market, are going to work with this idea of trade analytics and big data to get it done. This can help them to make some of the predictions that they need and will ensure that they are able to really finish up a trade and make a big profit.

This industry is also going to heavily rely on big data to help out with risk analytics, including fraud, risk management, anti-money laundering and more. In some instances, this has been used to help the bank or the financial institution figure out if they are going to lend money to an individual or not and can speed up the loan processing time very quickly.

Entertainment, Media, and Communications

While this may not be the first place where we are going to see the use of data and data analysis, these industries are going to work with them quite a bit.

Organizations that fall under this umbrella are going to simultaneously analyze the customer data that they have, along with some of the behavioral data in order to help create some customer profiles that are pretty detailed. They are then able to use these profiles in order to help them:

1. Create the content that is needed based on the different target audiences that they would like to reach.
2. It can help to recommend content on-demand in no time.
3. It can help us to measure content performance.

For example, we can look at the Wimbledon Championships. This was done thanks to YouTube Video and was able to leverage big data in order to deliver us with some detailed sentiment analysis on the tennis matches to web users, mobile users, and TV users, and it was able to do this all in real-time for us.

Then we can see it on the Spotify on-demand music service. This company has been able to work with the Hadoop big data analytics to help collect data from the millions of customers who work with them worldwide.

And then they would use this data in order to analyze it and give the best recommendations of music to the individual users who are on it.

Amazon Prime is on the list as well. This service is going to work in order to provide the best customer experience with the help of offering Kindle books, music, and videos in a one-stop-shop. And in order to figure out what to offer to their customers, what products to bring out next, and more, there is a lot of data analysis that will happen.

The Healthcare Industry

Some hospitals are even getting onto the idea of collecting data and using it for their needs as well. One hospital, Beth Israel, is using the data from a cell phone app, from millions of their patients, in order to allow the doctor to use evidence-based medicine as opposed to administering several medical and lab tests to all of the patients who head to the hospital. A battery of tests can be efficient, but you will find that this is not the most effective method to work with, and it can be really expensive for the patient.

Free public health data that we are able to look at and the Google Maps option is going to be used by the University of Florida in order to create visual data that is going to allow the healthcare professionals to identify issues faster, and will provide us with an efficient analysis of the healthcare information, used in tracking the spread of diseases that are chronic.

These are just a few of the methods that we will see in the healthcare industry working with this kind of analysis. They will use it to make a diagnosis of their patients, to help out with some of the more complex surgeries, and so much more overall. This is definitely a place where we are going to see a ton of changes in the near future as we work with more machine learning and data science.

Education

Big data is going to be used quite a bit when it comes to the world of higher education. One example of this is the University of Tasmania that is found in Australia. This college has 26,000 students and it has deployed what is known as a Learning and Management System that is able to track, along with some other things, when a system is logging into the system, how m much time they are spending on each of the pages that are found in the system, and the progress that the student is able to make over time.

To turn the tables a bit, we will find that this big data can be used to help measure how effective a teacher is when they interact with a student, and can ensure that the experience is as pleasant as possible between the teacher and the student. Teacher's performance can benefit from this because it can be fine-tuned based on the student numbers, subject matter, student demographics, student aspirations, behavioral classifications, and some other important variables as well.

Another place where we are able to see this show up is at the government level. The Office of Educational Technology in the U.S. Department of Education is using big data is to develop analytics to help correct the course students who are going astray while using some of the other online big data courses to help out with this. The click patterns are also going to be used in order to help detect when boredom is happening.

Natural Resources and Manufacturing

When we take a look at the natural resources industry, we will find that big data is going to allow us to have some predictive modeling in place. And this is a fantastic way to help us support some of the decision makings that are utilized for ingesting, and for helping us integrate a large amount of data from a lot of sources, including the temporal data, text, graphical data, and even geospatial data. Areas of interest where we are able to see this analysis come into play are going to be things like reservoir characterization and seismic interpretation.

Big data and the analysis that we are able to do with it has also been used on a frequent basis in order to help out with the issue of solving some of the major challenges that show up in the world of manufacturing, and to ensure that these companies are able to gain a bit competitive advantage over their competitors, along with a few other benefits that are present as well.

In addition, these companies have been able to work with the idea of machine learning and data analysis in order to really figure out where some of the waste in their company is found. This will ensure that we are able to figure out where the waste is, and how we can limit or eliminate it as much as possible along the way, reducing costs and increasing the profits found in the process.

Retail and Wholesale Trade

Working with big data and letting it drive some of the work that we are doing in the retail and wholesaling can make a big difference. When it comes to analyzing this data, we will find that we can learn about customer loyalty, POS, store inventory, the local demographics, and more. In the New York Big Show retail trade conference in 2014, some companies, including IBM, Cisco, and Microsoft, pitched the need to the retail industry of using all of this big data to help out with their analytics. And there were many other ways that these companies can work with this data including helping with:

1. Reducing the amount of fraud that was going on.
2. Optimized staffing through data from a lot of places like local events and some of the shopping patterns we have seen in the past.

3. Fast and timely analysis of the inventory that these retail companies have.

Social media has also brought up a lot of potentials when it comes to retail, but it is slowly being adopted by the brick and mortar stores. This can be a useful place to work on things like customer retention, promoting products, and getting new customers, all in one place.

Transportation

There are a lot of ways that we are able to work with big data, and put it through some of our data analysis tools when it comes to working with the industry of transportation. For example, some of these could be:

1. Governments are going to use this in many of the processes that they use with traffic. They can use the data, and the analysis, in order to help out with traffic control, intelligent transport systems, route planning, congestion management, and more.
2. The private sector can benefit, as well. they are able to use this to help out with a lot of tasks, including technological enhancements, revenue

management, logistics, and to ensure that they maintain their competitive advantage.

3. Individuals can also benefit from this process because they will use the idea of big data in order to help them with route planning. This can help them to save on time and fuel and for some of the travel arrangements in tourism.

As we can see, there are so many ways that we are able to use the data that we find in the real world and put it to good use in a lot of the companies and businesses that we see and utilize on a daily basis. When these companies are able to take all of that data and put it through a good data analysis, they are able to solve many of the problems that we have been talking about in this chapter, and really work on serving their customers in a more effective manner.

Conclusion

Thank you for making it through to the end of *Python for Data Analysis*, let's hope it was informative and able to provide you with all of the tools you need to achieve your goals whatever they may be.

The next step is to get started with your very own data analysis right away. There are so many businesses and industries that are able to benefit when it comes to working with this kind of process, that it makes sense that your company would be able to benefit as well. Working on one of these data analysis, and some of the other steps that we took some time to explore in this guidebook, is one of the best ways to learn more about your business, about the customers who want to shop with you, how your competition is handling things, and even about the market. Overall, when you ask the right questions and work with data analysis in the proper manner, it is going to ensure that you can make smart decisions that bring your business to the future.

This guidebook took some time to look more at the idea of data analysis and what you are able to do with it. This is kind of the exciting part that comes with data analysis because we get to take all of the great information that we have been able to gather in other steps, and we get to clean it off and send it through some of the algorithms that we would like to use in order to find the patterns and insights that are inside of them. This allows us to learn a lot more about our business and can give us insights that we can't get from other methods.

And that is what this guidebook is all about. We took the time to explore the idea of data analysis and how we are able to use this for some of our own needs as well. We get to explore what this analysis is all about, how it is going to work, and even some of the different steps that are going to show up with this if we would like to work with it. And that is what makes it so amazing. It comes with a lot of steps that we have to keep track of, but when we are able to do this, it is going to ensure that our business gets ahead of the rest.

We also took it further and looked at how we are able to work with the Python language to make all of this work for our needs, and even how we are able to learn more with machine learning, how to create some of the different algorithms that are important to this process and more. And at the end, we looked at why the idea of data visuals are going to be important here, and how we are able to make them work for some of our needs when really seeing how the data plays out for us.

There are so many different parts that are going to come with a good data analysis that we are trying to work with. And learning how these can come together to provide us with good patterns, predictions, and insights in order to get the best results that we would like. When you are ready to see what a data science project is able to do for your business, and you would like to learn more about how to complete your own data analysis to get these insights out of all the data, make sure to check out this guidebook to help you get started.

Finally, if you found this book useful in any way, a review on Amazon is always appreciated!